THE WOMAN ON THE SHORE

DATE DUE

The Enchanted Echo, 1944
Pressed on Sand, 1955
Emu, Remember!, 1956
The Crafte So Long To Lerne, 1959
The Blur in Between: Poems 1960–61, 1962
Poems for All the Annettes, 1962; rev. ed. 1968; 3d ed. 1973
The Cariboo Horses, 1965
North of Summer, 1967
Wild Grape Wine, 1968
Love in a Burning Building, 1970
The Quest for Ouzo, 1971
Hiroshima Poems, 1972
Selected Poems, 1972
On the Bearpaw Sea, 1973
Sex & Death, 1973
In Search of Owen Roblin, 1974
The Poems of Al Purdy: A New Canadian Library Selection, 1976
Sundance at Dusk, 1976
A Handful of Earth, 1977
At Marsport Drugstore, 1977
No Other Country [prose], 1977
Moths in the Iron Curtain, 1978
No Second Spring, 1978
Being Alive: Poems 1958–78, 1978
The Stone Bird, 1981
Bursting into Song: An Al Purdy Omnibus, 1982
Birdwatching at the Equator, 1983
Morning and It's Summer, 1984
The Bukowski/Purdy Letters 1964–1974 [prose], 1984
Piling Blood, 1984
Selected Poems [in Russian translation], 1986
The Collected Poems of Al Purdy, 1986

The Woman on the Shore

poems by

Al Purdy

M&S

Canadian Cataloguing in Publication Data

Purdy, Al, 1918-
  The woman on the shore

Poems.
ISBN 0-7710-7217-1

I. Title.

PS8531.U73W6 1990   C811'.54   C89-090772-2
PR9199.3.P87W6 1990

The publisher would like to thank the Ontario Arts Council for its
assistance.

The author would like to thank Sam Solecki and Bernice Eisenstein
for their help.

A number of these poems were first published, some in slightly revised
form, in the following: *The Ant's Forefoot, Books in Canada, The
Canadian Forum, Canadian Women's Studies, The Second Macmillan
Anthology, The Malahat Review, Saturday Night;* some were
broadcast on the CBC.

Set in Pilgrim by The Typeworks, Vancouver

Printed and bound in Canada

McClelland & Stewart Inc.
The Canadian Publishers
481 University Avenue
Toronto, Ontario M5G 2E9

For Norma, Eunice, and Judy

This is my chance to say Hello to anyone who might have
picked up this book, or possible friends who've read my stuff for
more than the first time. So—: greetings to the crowd in the
phone booth.

The last ten poems call for explanation. Some of them come
from out-of-print books, somehow overlooked when Russell
Brown and I were preparing my *Collected Poems* for the
printer. Others are from magazines, and have never appeared in
books. One poem, "Ulysses Alone," has reverted to its
magazine title. The speaker in "Schoolmaster's Song" is
fictional; but I'm real, and I said it. And I like to think the kid
in "Vera Cruz Hotel" is also me. (Years later, that memory of
the boy sitting on the bed gives me a very queer feeling.)
Consuelo, in "The Apotheosis of Miss Monroe," is real to me in
a way the sex goddess never was. "Scott Hutcheson's Boat,"
reconstructed by Angus Mowat, is now resting at The Marine
Museum of the Great Lakes in Kingston, Ontario. And all my
children have left me.

Sam Solecki and I ransacked old magazines and out-of-print
books for those last poems; and I do appreciate Sam's verbal
restraint, since he will be editing the sentence I am now
writing. I hadn't expected to be writing it after my *Collected
Poems* appeared, but life and death are full of surprises.

I heard or thought I did
before I died
the other pilot's shadow far below
whisper in fear and amazement
Achtung! Achtung Spitfire!

(Falling
drifting down forever under the parachute
I heard enchanted mutterings
and felt light-headed from my wound
I said: "The rest of the way alone please"
and someone beside me nodded
in the darkness...)

Milord I plead extenuating circumstances
I was young so very young
it was all such an adventure for me
I was Lancelot in the skyblue forest
I thought my heart was pure
but looking down at the burning cities
after the bombs fell
I am not so sure

The med officer unwrapped black rubber hose
from my arm like a cold snake
I looked at him expectantly
with raging excitement
he said "No"

Therefore:
no pilot-navigator-gunner I
peering from plastic nose cone
all is illusion all is sham
I live on and on in my mundane lives

which do not include any of the above
and I am not so young
dreams of Spitfire Hurricane Flying Fort
vanish pft-pft
no unmusical mutter of machine guns
assaults the high blue
and fifty years have plodded by
since I wept for the sky
I sink to lowest of the low
I salute civilians
AC2 AC2 AC2*

*Aircraftsman Second Class is
the lowest rank in the RCAF

CONTENTS

I

3 The Gift of a Water-Colour
4 The Prison Lines at Leningrad
5 Quetzal Birds
6 Horses
8 Vertical Versus Horizontal
10 The Darkness
11 Seven Ways of Looking at Something Else
13 Voyeur
15 Cartography
17 Barn Burning
19 A Handle for Nothingness
25 Jalopies
28 Red Leaves
29 Riding West
33 Freight Train Murder
37 Orchestra
39 Memo to the Unemployment Insurance Commission
41 Papyrus
42 Herodotus of Halicarnassus
45 Dog and Hummingbird
47 A God in the Earth
50 In a Dry Season
51 On the Flood Plain
53 The Others
55 Lok
57 One Moth Is like Any Other
58 On the Death of F.R. Scott
61 Lady
62 I Think of John Clare
64 Questions
65 An Arrogance
67 Maybe Fish
69 For Margaret

71 Lawrence to Laurence
73 Flying over Vancouver Island
75 Letter to Morley Callaghan
78 Called on Accounta Rain
80 Everything We Could Imagine
81 The Woman on the Shore
83 Springtime
84 Gradations
85 In the Desert
87 Yellow Primavera in Mexico
89 The Gossamer Ending

II

93 In Peace Memorial Park
95 Scott Hutcheson's Boat
98 Return from Kikastan
100 Over the Sierra Maestras
102 On the Apotheosis of Miss Monroe
104 Vera Cruz Hotel
107 Ulysses Alone
108 The Liars
110 Beer Poem
112 Schoolmaster's Song

I

A place I ought to know
English Bay and Kitsilano
long yellow grass in the foreground
and mountains farther away–
Myself so sentimental
I think of an unimportant
man standing painting one day
seriously and with respect for all
those others who painted
their trivia and minutiae
judging the morning
into their colours
deciding the sky's
blue translation
onto a few inches
        of wood-pulp
Going home afterwards
soaked in blue
the fierce concentration
        unslaked
going home for six years
since 1957
keeping it that long that many
unpossessed mornings
        then
                giving it away

1963

THE PRISON LINES AT LENINGRAD
—for Anna Akhmatova

She speaks for them
             —the speechless dead:
the woman in her chill misery
who said, "Could you describe this?"
Akhmatova answering, "Yes."

They led her husband off like a dog,
already emptiness in his heart
—in hers the poems since, a song
that echoes in soundless prison yards.

Number 300—is she still here,
mourning husband, mourning child?
—the Neva's ice-choked water spares
no swimmer, cannot hear their cries.

The Peterhof in Baltic mist,
and Peter's statue in greenish bronze;
Stalin inside the Kremlin walls
drills unhearing firing squads.

The Tsars arise to cheer themselves,
that's Nicholas who used to wed the bed;
and hand on hip, standing negligently,
a man with ice pick in his head.

Siberia—the name like an anthem,
is requiem for millions dead;
no Mozart here with his last breath
to choir an immense Russian sadness...

"Far from your ocean, Leningrad,
I leave my body"—they heard the cry,
those prisoners, their anthem hers:
earth speaks as if earth were alive.

They exist somewhere between yes and no
that three-foot tail has elements of both
I have not really seen green till now
sea-leaf-emerald dire-jade-jealousy green
so imploded and concentrated one hears
it chunking at the soul's rear window

Only chiefs might wear those tail feathers
not dukes duchesses belted earls
                              just Kings
—in another life on the hot dry plains of Anahuac
I have seen thousands waiting—the commoners
Aztec Mixtec Toltec Mayan unemotional
unquestioning yearning they-know-not-what
faces like scabbards of swords

I knew a guy once would buy a single drop
of perfume worth a trillion bucks
for a girl he knew on the next block
—the quetzal is like that
one glimpse
dipping above the well at Chichen Itza
skimming the sorrowful deserts of Yucatan
and troubled haciendas of Guatamala
this non-Christian-Muslim atheist deity
squeezes the heart

HORSES

—stand beside yourself
your other self
the waiting child
in an imaginary town
and nobody there no one
except the dead
everyone dead
except—

And they'd come
you knew they'd come
out of empty streets
into the sun
my quick steppers my thunder-footed
ones wearing all shades of copper
gold umber satin-covered grey
and black tar babies shining
and me in my plural child's disguise
watching them
in calm sun watching
the wild eye in its rolling heavens

These were the steady cloppers
these were the prancers
going whusp-whusp-whusp all four
feet together like one alone
and I was a witness
in the whispery winter morning
with the shadow beside me
being born over and over
every day outside the warm house
every blink of the eye

Moving to market and slaughter
of ducks and upside-down chickens
in summer the dainty ones
with clover breath
every step a dance step
their feet loved each other
their feet were lovers
before the road was paved
and the great beasts came

(They are of course dog food
and cat feed long since
while the planet cycle
repeats and repeats and vultures over
my head are cancer-stroke-heart disease
but I pay no attention
now is parenthesis
now is going backward)

—and sometimes when I was older
I ran beside them a little
way and they knew they knew
eye blinkers notwithstanding
they knew the small boy
they remembered they remembered
my quick steppers my thunder-footed
ones wearing gold and silver
jewellery brother and sister
to the wind and jingle jingle
in cold weather went the bells
went the years went the child
all the way to the world's edge
all the way home

—and the body-clock ticks on

Never mind why
pay no attention to when
only that it did happen
—that little mammal sucking
dinosaur eggs at early dawn
trying to figure out a new method
for safecracking those eggs
and leaving the burglary undetectable
—that minuscule creature
with beady treacherous eyes
stood suddenly upright
and proclaimed his own importance
in a series of one-decibel shrieks
no self-respecting carnivore
even noticed

Think more on the matter
be advised in anthropogenesis jargon
that when the lil bugger stood upright
his position relative to the world
changed to right angles with the horizon
(in geometry preferred term is "perpendicular")
and in the first employment of admass
became "the far-seeing one"
before such language was
in general usage

The advantages of verticality were several:
lower vegetation—ferns and such
small shrubbery—could be looked above
danger glimpsed while still far-distant
and it was really marvellous for the ego
While gentle ungulates grazed
and remained belly-plumb with earth
and the carnivores made rude noises

but stayed horizontal
The far-seeing one remained upright
and praised his own perspicacity
and forgot that other world

Remember the morning?
—our shadows long in the long grass
our bodies swift in the leaping distance
how we overtook our own beginnings
in sweetness of dew and morning
and so still we heard god's heartbeat
in the wet near earth

Remember the noonday?
—the trees were green sentinels
and birds warned us of danger
and we raced the west wind over the grasslands
and discovered the east wind in earth's turning
in springtime everything was shining
as if it had just been born
and it had been

Remember the evening?
—how it was in that great blaze of sun
horizon embroidery
blue green purple orange mixed with blackness
being born as a colour
asking ourselves who we were
and knowing anyway
—and quietness in the forest
when leaves talked together
and the words they said
were sleep sleep sleep
and we slept
our bodies joined to each other
and were parallel with the earth
—we slept
and dreamed a strange dream
and woke and were not ourselves

THE DARKNESS

1

It cuts down the number of *things*
in the world
decreases visible objects
there aren't so many people
things get rarer
                gain value

2

−that other world
the little-known one
        without horizons
where those who sleep by day
and those who sleep by night
meet briefly in the false dawn
and do not believe
               in each other

SEVEN WAYS OF LOOKING AT
SOMETHING ELSE

The colour that glances off
from another colour
looks at something else
aslant and tangential
and may not be seen alone
only in symbiosis
—rings around necks of certain birds
to see that not-blue and not-green
requires growing an extra space
in your head to keep them safe in
—followed this girl into a museum
standing by a mummy-case
waiting for the sun on painted queen
at that moment watching the girl
watching the queen watching the watcher
unable to break the circle
—in the Mediterranean off Famagusta
sunken bronze and filigree gold memories
have taken the sun to bed on the sea bottom
solar fires burn in mud
and the sea-moan crying in lava caves
Greek women not crying for their lovers
aching for their doodads
—take for instance
that planet they figured out
had to be there on accounta how
the others acted because of it
like a dancer with invisible partner

Give me that final mystery
the invisible woman so lovely

she is beyond my conception of her
yet only possible because of me
sweet shadow in the bedroom
my rebellious beloved satellite orbiting me
yearning to be free

Watching "our creek" below the house
(the map shows it but doesn't name it)
this separate slice of wilderness
a green pleat below the pavement
protected salmon-spawning waters
concealed at the city's outer limits
Me an eastern exile
watching the rarity of western snow
and white gets written on quickly
birds scribble signatures
a sleek sea otter from Georgia Strait
swims under the highway culvert
at high tide every morning
—here he is now
romping in from the sea

Farther inland
the creek swirls under two more highways
at Victoria Airport its water-birth
is private and covered over by concrete
a safe distance from runways
and roaring Vancouver arrivals

Under our window
a duck flirts with its water portrait
the otter enjoys being what an otter is
and squirms and rolls over in snow
contorts like a circus performer
unselfconscious
does everything but balance a ball
on its nose and would if he had one
Watching the otter I think of all that joy
in living so rarely seen in people

—downtown faces on Government Street
scrunched with bad temper in snow
people hidden inside their steel boxes
driving home wanting to hurt something

What have we lost
—or did we ever have it?
—the otter's squirming explosion of joy
at being so alive champagne bubbles
pop in his birthday whiskers
But I think: who in his right mind
would want to be an otter?

Upstream
a duck dives for the excellent provender
our creek provides at breakfast
it occurs to me that duck has grown careless
stayed at the same spot too long
and the otter is nowhere in sight
I turn away
remembering the remains of blood banquets
noticed on this tranquil shoreline
a kingfisher watching
a cat from the neighbouring house
turn away while it's still idyllic
make a sandwich for lunch
use the bathroom
watch for blood in the stool

–the plains–a little west of Calgary
where the land humps up in waves
like a brown sea
before there was a railway before roads
the shape of things is the same
–and something about the tilt of land there
the Bow River running eastward
a hawk circling high enough
to see over most mountains
but not these
something that said this is here

The sun a projectile aimed straight down
at noon and man the target
you'd think a man ought to feel small
being one-millionth of nothing small
but doesn't
occupying such a large chunk of creation
and himself a transient
he can claim everything and nothing

I'm trying to say I'd know this place
even when dreaming–the misted mountains
that sometimes pretend they're not there
then the mind achieves the *idea* of stone
which is indestructible
–the rain an infinity of rain here
and snow the basic mathematics of snow
you can't conceive these hills
in any but their own terms
–someone who has wandered there
and seen in the snow
the feet of some small animal

whose tracks had crossed and recrossed
his own for centuries

Something about the tilt of land
I'd know
but I don't know how I'd know

BARN BURNING

Stayed up late
working on a prose piece
around 2 a.m.
when a great light bulged in at the windows
and peered at what I was writing
making it trivial

I drove there
half a mile away
in a kind of anxiety
for I don't know what
maybe fear of the red monster
I parked at a safe distance
while cops prowled around like sleepwalkers
dreaming of arson
with blank expressions
acting like they were needed somewhere else
while the planet burned

It was more than a fire
it was Genesis with a safety match
it was the Destroying Angel with a Bic lighter
—a worm of fear chewed my guts
but I wasn't afraid
it was an exaltation
a shiver at the edge of extinction
a godhead of transience

Meanwhile back at the barn
whiskered whirlwinds climbed the sky
fifty-foot timbers barn-boards steel spikes
and tons of nightmares
became weightless auroras

I stared higher:
the Big Dipper the North Star the
planets dangling like grapes
in a galactic vineyard
and even the home galaxy I'm standing on
all vanished
and words lost their connectives

I suppose it was "important" for me
to keep looking at
everything else diminished
including certainly myself
I went home and slept
and asked my questions in sleep
In the morning words returned
and the sun from a nest of clouds
and little diamonds of dew
sparkled in the pale white light
that filtered into my mind
and the clichés were restful
they made common sense

Man
defined as *Homo sapiens*
supposedly intelligent
once a rat-sized creature
in the late Cretaceous
sixty-five million years ago
whose brain got itchy and
suddenly outgrew its body
developed memory
called things by names
and contrived a phantom
self glimpsing a phantom
self somewhere inside
a cosmic cornflakes box
wandering the star roads
crying out lonesomely
"Hail Brother–Hail Camerado"
and shit like that
or else "Fuck you Bub"
which has decidedly
serious implications
re social harmony
and peaceful coexistence
for the rat-like species

However:
think of space
I mean deep space
fifteen billion years
after the "Big Bang"
of astronomic theory
–the farthest galaxies
of our one and only
universe exploding

outward at speeds of
"hundreds of millions
of miles an hour–"
(did nothing *im*plode?)
Beyond the outermost
edges of these galaxies
nothing
literally nothing
However
I conceive a quantum
leap of the mind
beyond the outermost
edge of the universe
therefore
a fractional me
after-image on retina
faint sound of here
projection of smell
exists out there
in deep space
thru an act of will
definite as an act
of the body and once
this willed me is
brought into existence
it cannot not be and
neither affirms nor
denies: is is is
in that sense immortal–:
Call him Sur
Sur for SurroGate

(Brief pause
to catch your breath
for just a moment
and think of him
abstractly again)
Man:

(the sexual plural)
a kind of mad inventor
with grandiose dreams
of wish-fulfilment
but practical sometimes
his mind makes pictures
of things before things
exist the brain sends
signals and he watches
a hand move he
observes the hand
writing and inside-out
blueprints materialize
—sometimes his electro-
magnetic thoughts may
even touch London or
Paris or next door
moons of Jupiter
sending traces of mind
minute unmeasurable
ghost molecules of
the sedentary self
travelling into known
places while the space-
ship brain sleeps
in its bone hangar

Meanwhile
Sur moves outward
in black emptiness
just a few light years
ahead of exploding
galaxies
—he is of course
quite unprovable
to himself or anyone
else—a concept only
signifying nothing

Time which is
a series of events
monitored by clicks
of clocks and planetary
seasons and flow of blood
to the brain does not
exist there except
for Sur
Distance itself
does not exist there
because nothing else
exists but Sur
And if we postulate
love and hate
(such human emotions)
they don't exist either
and the works of man
are absent which
leaves very little

At the outermost edge
of the farthest galaxies
Sur floats calmly
and having free will
decides to speed up
moves farther and farther
out into nothing
which is not quite
nothing because of Sur
He can't communicate
or think as such
no word or thought
to his alter-ego
in fact he is himself only
a detached thought
island entity
And he can't televise
back some discovery

from the great emptiness
—say there may be
other remote galaxies
trillions of light years
farther out
and there may not

(Pause again to
consider the conceptual
animal Man:
who conceives love
out of need to justify
sex and comfort loneliness
but cannot prove love
nor even himself
except as intangible word
a word meaning weakness or
strength if you prefer
—who imagines God
with a long white beard
fatherly not motherly
and fearsomely kind
rewarding good conduct
with an eternity
of boredom)

Of course there may
actually be a
god out there
in that black distance
and equally
there may not
(He is unprovable
but lack of evidence
is evidence *against*)
and beyond the universe
beyond learned theories
the conceptual being

of Sur exists
his minus molecules
sail on sail on
(Whitman notwithstanding)
Nothing out there
but even nothing
has being in our minds
if we name it
refer to it
use it for thought
then nothing is something
you could look it up
in any dictionary
As for Sur
this conceived being:
once set in motion
lack of evidence against
is evidence *for*
And thus and so
in inconceivable null
(which is obviously
perfectly conceivable)
Sur exists:
add the rest of him
add the last syllable
add the "Gate"
as an opening
a door to somewhere
an aperture
an entrance
–Goodbye

JALOPIES

That '27 Whippet
was my first
I used to watch
the occasional Rolls
ocean-going size
chauffeur-driven
with built-in blondes
and wonder how it would
be to drive my nuts
and bolts Bang
into that shark grille
(but I drove it bang
instead into a
garbage truck on
Dundas St. Trenton
Later a '37 Ford
with fish gills
and I wondered again
how it would be to
nibble the paint off
Packards and Caddys
too if edible
Not jealousy no
not ever jealousy
raw nose pressed
on rich man's wind-
shield wipers
Maybe envy
just a little
on accounta the
standard equipment
of those four-
wheeled bedrooms:

brunettes
blondes et cetera
displayed as jewellery
laid out like booty
languid in upholstery
prone on leather
and were themselves
upholstery
And those business men
who told the girls
with fatherly fondling
they'd adorn soon
their very own
pre-paid apartments
Undoubtedly many
guys like me
staring lustfully
at soft redheads
and various other
bottled shades
of girls who never
parked in back lanes
or lonely places
near water moons
only always
in heated limos
in front of jewellers

I think they knew
those dead business
men how we felt
me and those other
envious pragmatists
with starving noses
and various other
anatomic fragments
pressed on windshields

And therefore:
all you chauvinists
xenophobic bastards
of atheist persuasion
and Marxist leanings
revolutionaries
in short shit
disturbers of all kinds
hearken
to my song
and please lay off
I beg you
my new Mercury

—all over the earth
little fires starting up
especially in Canada
some yellow leaves too
buttercup and dandelion yellow
dancing across the hillside
I say to my wife
"What's the yellowest thing there is?"
"School buses"
—a thousand school buses are double-
parked on 401 all at once

I suppose this is the one thing
your average level-headed Martian
or Venusian could not imagine
about Earth:
                    red leaves
and the way humans attach emotion
to one little patch of ground
and continually go back there
in the autumn of our lives
to deal with some of the questions
that have troubled us
on our leapfrog trip thru the Universe
for which there are really no answers
except at this tranquil season
of falling leaves
watching them a kind of jubilation
sometimes mistaken for sadness

Kicked off the freight train
at Vernon B.C.
in the Okanagan Valley
we walked the highway
lined with ripe cherry trees
—on the sidewalks of towns
ripe young girls
pretending they didn't see us
their fathers no doubt with shotguns
near at hand
their mothers peering
behind lace curtains
mouths twisted unpleasantly
and who could blame them
Jim and I
bums both of us
stopped one night
to sleep in a sawmill
snored into cedar shavings
dreamt I was a tree
and dreamt of girls
In Penticton
people on the streets
looked at you
as if your mother
was a whore and you
her pimp
Jim laughed
and I laughed
but it wasn't funny
and we watched the girls
and the sun watched them
and their mothers watched them

until they blushed
and looked away
all but the ones
who didn't
One job
on the valley highway
shovelling gravel
over hot wet tar
till the sun blinded us
and we laughed
and drank gallons
of cold Okanagan water
Then a car smashed
the stop sign and
nearly killed us
and the foreman bawled
the guy into guilty silence
and we stood watching
not laughing
Another job
for a guy named Skimmerhorn
—it sounded like that
anyway—a kraut farmer
near Kelowna
in the mountains
the low mountains
maybe a mile high
I never measured
Me 17
Jim 20
In the bunkhouse
(three shithouses joined)
we played John McCormack
and Wilf Carter yodelled
"Oh That Strawberry Roan"
on the windup gramophone
And worked felling timber

with crosscut saws
splitting it with wedges
forking hay onto a truck
in the high grasslands
sunup to sundown
It was a dead end
for both of us
that mountain farm
I wanted to keep going west
to the salt chuck
a job on the fishing boats
and leaping salmon
that rattled cans
on the grocery shelf
Jim wanted to stay
work for a stake
"make something of himself"
I left him there
sawing down trees
and splitting the trunks
forking hay for Skimmerhorn
a guy with a face
like a hundred-year-old lemon
Before leaving
he cheated me of half
the wages he'd promised
and I argued
but I went

Jim
angry with me
for leaving
and sad also:
we shook hands
and my throat choked
at feeling
what you couldn't say

and didn't have
words for it
anyway
in the mountain silence
being 17
for the last time
and some inside part
of myself waking up
and crying out
in the silence

Killing a man
it kinda bothers one
—and leave off
that "one" stuff
I mean me
but did I
or didn't I?

Riding into Vancouver
between boxcars
braced against couplings
in 1935
—guts aching
from not eating much
weight 170
burned black and red from sun
I was a story
happening to me
Vancouver
—mills belching smoke
sawdust and fish smell
the griminess of things
and cops
waiting in yards
to break your arms
bums waiting
to steal your money
if you had any
—in the streets
your own face
in store windows
was a dirty bum's
was someone else
the skeezix body

a skinny mosquito's
and nobody looking
knew me was *me*
I suppose
I've delayed saying it
anyway:
just one day in Vancouver
then an eastbound freight
lazy couplings banging
slow at level crossing
in downtown Vancouver
grabbing boxcar ladder
cops elsewhere
but wanting you gone
from their town
their clean city
and I went–
Into the mountains
braced between fir timbers
on a rumbling flatcar
and cold oh cold
I was a long drink of water
zero all the way down
but not alone
Someone behind me
in the freezing dark
reached for my cock
I pushed him off
and he went
then came back
I pushed him again
hard
but he kept coming
that hand kept reaching
into the darkness

A gentle man
no doubt he was

and kind to his mother
but growing stronger
more insistent
and certainly not
to be ignored
I wound myself
into a tight bundle
a coiled spring
feet against him
the invader
and exploded myself
a flesh bomb
a bone projectile
and it felt like
killing a chicken
In howling wind
of the train's passage
I heard him going
or imagined it
in my timber castle
—a thud and a cry
receding somewhere
but where it was
he went to
has no maps

For a long time
I didn't get to sleep
and questioned myself
without any answers
while the train
went hooting eastward
thru stone canyons
to the prairies
And five days later
near Regina
still wondering
whether to feel guilty

or not
and writing this
fifty years later
wondering whether
it matters. . .

They do not know where their bodies are
their flesh has fled
inside the blonde cello
into warm red darkness
of the cherry-coloured violin
—and they are looking for their souls
bent over the crooked instruments
jagged shapes of sound
sheep-gut and horsehair
wire drawn thin as the tingle
of the seeking heart
that says "I want to know you"
See now
they are looking for their souls
and they are outside time
which is to say
their body-clocks have stopped
they have forgotten
wives husbands lovers
the cry of human gender
in one tumescent moment
solemn as eternity's
endless et cetera

None of all this do they know
not consciously
the space between thoughts
expanded to forever
where music is a continuous silence
except for the slight
"ping" sound of the absolute
—and when that other silence
applause begins
bodies are restored

souls unnecessary
doorknobs open doors
manhole covers murmur
buttons enter buttonholes
beasts die at the slaughterers
and the silver hiatus
ends

Came back from Europe broke
hitch-hiked west
to Vancouver
bearded and dirty
knocked on the door
at 6 a.m.
and she hardly knew me
I could see the indecision
whether to allow
this guy in her bed
or kick him down Kingsway
or call the cops
it was touch and go
for at least five seconds
I got a job at Grange Mattress
on 2nd near Cambie
bluffing a little
telling Andy Grange
I could run every
machine in the place
and I did
almost—
Rode the roll-edge
like a cowboy
on a hunchback horse
aimed the tufting machine
like a killer crossbow
had everyone fooled
but me
And I must've decided
about then
I was no longer
a loser
—that trip to the Hebrides

and the Paris Left Bank
the vineyard country
of France
had changed something
in fact
changed quite a lot
And watching all
the blue-collar boys
the 8 to 5ers
off to work like slaves
over rain-grey streets
the 9 to 5ers an hour later
bosses in bed till noon
I thought what the hell
and quit my job again
bundled wife and kid
into the old Chevy
with a hole in the muffler
and started for Montreal
The curious thing
about all this
is what happened
to my insides
—how did my discontent
then become
my discontent now
along with maybe
some added ingredients?
I don't know
but just the same
I'd do it again
quit every damn job
including the last one
and finally become
as I am now
unemployable
by God

I've grown old
with a thousand
or so photographs
of you circulating
in my blood
—a little camera
in the limbic brain
took those pictures
at different ages
of your own life
They are pumped
to far places
of the body
returning and returning
—a small child
smiling shyly
a slim teenager
with brown eyes
a young woman
with an expression
that melts the heart
The morning rivers
and even lakes
calm backwaters
of the roving blood
say your name to me

This fever in the veins
        this running fire
flickering on the sea
this rumour on the wind
in Ephesus Babylon Persepolis
this whisper in the night
about murdered kings
            —is news?

Belshazzar's overthrow
riding the backs of dolphins
across the sea from Asia
            —is news?

No presses roll
no harried editor snarls
Where? When? Who? How?
                only
a mild-mannered middle-aged observer
listener rather than talker
quietly deciding what he really thinks
about things other people have
already decided
staring bemused among sleepy herdsmen
near a mountain village at Thurii
wandering the agora at Athens

He fantasizes headlines:
PERICLES IN CROOKED LAND DEAL (No!)
AGAMEMNON A YELLOW COWARD (Very unlikely)
CROESUS CONSULTS DELPHIC ORACLE (True)
XERXES FLOGS HELLESPONT WITH WHIPS
WHEN WATER REFUSES OBEDIENCE
(Informant swears truth of this
on his honour—which may be insufficient)

42

News of Wars:
Thousands dead on battlefields
Wolves feast on torn bodies
Children die of starvation
The world a desert...
Why?

He considers the recent past:
Nicaea Salamis Marathon   Thermopylae
Xerxes and the Persians
invading Greece
Headline: WE WIN
(sub-heading)
WE KNOCK HELL OUTA THE PERSIANS
but why–*why* did we win?
Consider some reasons:
–the phalanx?
sterling character of Greek hoplites?
leadership of Leonidas and Themistocles?
But I say the ships
that old man on the docks
muttering to himself
(interview him later)
"Three banks of oars much
superior to double row of oars"
(seems logical)
that doddering old shipwright
who invented triremes
–a new design
paid for with Greek silver
–paid for with death
one always pays for victories

But why Greeks and Persians?
Well now
it's like we got into bad habits
and kept kidnapping each other's women
until someone's husband

got really annoyed
—that might be one Why

A reasonable man
listening to what people say
in the marketplace
at peddlers' stalls
at the docks talking to fishermen
off-shift miners
ploughmen in springtime
taking notes and considering...

(For gawd's sake
they're talking about a statue
on the main street
for the old bastard
I mean why?
—that sloppy old man
staring at women's legs
wine-bibber
"old father of lies"
buttonholing everyone
asking the world questions...)

Quietly in a vineyard at Thurii
Herodotus
dreams life never ends
—in the Islands of the Blest
of the Western Sea
all his loves waiting
the fair and not so fair
the dark ones with lips like flames
their faces shining on him
their eyes like springs of light
Let it be so!

Our canoe grated on gravel beach
of an island in Cumberland Sound
–Jonahsie and Leah unloaded things
I hoisted a blind husky bitch
with milky eyes and four pups
onto the beach feeling like a midwife
(later I got the same job twice more
the dog beginning to trust me)
For much of that summer evening
on an island at the world's edge
hunters on the high black cliffs
fired at seals in water below
and icebergs like fancy wedding cakes
drifted past in a dream
I lay in my sleeping bag
thinking about what it was like
to be a blind dog on Baffin Island
or to be blind anywhere
as my own darkness closed around me

Years later at Ameliasburg
a hummingbird got inside our garage
–thumbnail or peachstone size
iridescent blue shoulders
blurred invisible wings skittering
up and down the plate-glass window
frantically rising and falling
trying to reach the real outdoors
instead of this phony outdoors
I called my wife
thinking my big hands might do damage
she took the bird in both her hands
like holding it in a cradle
and gave it a gift of the world

I remembered that blind dog
and hopefully without undue moralizing
thinking
if life is never a shower of diamonds
and rainbows avoid your own vicinity
there is a "connectedness" about things
enabling a relay runner ahead or behind you
to hand over the baton of memory
from one person to another
whereby a blind dog and hummingbird
in lieu of diamonds and rainbows
may go whirling into the future

King St. Laurent Diefenbaker Pearson Trudeau
Clark and again Trudeau
the names make little tinkles in history
they rhyme with faker and fearful and bark and no
look them up in books
to find out what they accomplished
very little
And Mulroney the last of them
a man who loves his friends
so much he loves the country
less and less
and gives it away free to Americans
The god in the earth does not know them
the earth-god has other business

The old names have died
vanished from memory
Macdonald Durham McGee Cartier
the builders
who moved men to hate and love
in the light of flaming ballot boxes
their banners danced in the hearts of men
And now the economic terrorists
call the star-spangled tune
in Ottawa

Was it Poundmaker who knew
Wandering Spirit and Dumont
was it those who perceived beyond shadow
talked to the god in the earth
accepted his fruits
made their peace with men
and died knowing?

Was it the explorers
Mackenzie   Fraser   Tyrrell   Hearne
Radisson   La Salle   and   La Verendrye
who yoked themselves to horizons
glimpsed far distance from their doorways
and leaped the intervening space
before dying?

Perhaps Mackenzie the rebel
had some conception of it
or Papineau's men with pitchforks
and bloody bandages in potato fields
struggling to articulate with bodies
what their hearts realized?
Or was there no one in past time
for whom the nation became much more
than brown parentheses
between blue oceans?

But   King   St. Laurent   Diefenbaker   Pearson   Trudeau
Clark and again Trudeau
and Mulroney who loves Americans
and wants them to vote for him
—meaningless names
men who accomplished little
and latterly failed
without even knowing they failed
What shall we think of them
these small men
who cannot lift the heart
or stir the blood with visions
a direction an aim
if not for the sky then for the earth
the earth that is more than earth
—unaware that history will judge them
as it judges all of us
for littleness for blindness
and not with love

The earth-god does not know them
has commerce with sun and rain
birth and death and the spirit
and the land that is eternal
there is no time
for faker and fearful and bark and no
and that other little man
who found his friends in Washington
and lost his own country
The earth-god does not know them
the god in the earth has other business

The juices inside women's bodies
are the condiments of heaven and earth
whose formulae remain secret in the skulls of dead alchemists
Those woman-juices
must well from springs deep inside earth
they are the unimaginable and certainly unwritten
proof that a god or gods do exist as corollary
to unseen orchids waiting to be stepped on
by men with cork helmets in imaginary jungles
—a young god who has discovered in unmapped regions
of Venus this shimmering source
of all his questions about death and life hereafter
the answer that contains always its own opposite
and circles back on itself to become a question
—and the young god being celibate
must wander mad across parched deserts of earth
until the great rains come
—and Jesus wept

Midnight:
it's freezing on the lake
and wind whips ice eastward
but most of the water remains open
—and stars visit earth
tumbled about like floating candles
on the black tumulus
then wind extinguishes the silver fire
but more flash down
and even those reflections reflect
on the sides of waves
even the stars' reflections reflect stars

Ice:
far older than earth
primordial as the Big Bang
—cold unmeasured by Celsius and Fahrenheit
quarrelling about it on a Jurassic shingle
—before Pangaea and Gondwanaland
arrive here in the 20th century
born like a baby
under the flashlight beam
Bend down and examine the monster
and freeze for your pains
—tiny oblong crystals
seem to come from nowhere
little transparent piano keys
that go tinkle tinkle tinkle
while the wind screams
—and you feel like some shivering hey
presto god grumbling at his fucked-up weather
hurry indoors hurry indoors to heaven

People have told us we built too near the lake
"The flood plain is dangerous" they said
and no doubt they know more about it than we do
—but here wind pressed down on new-formed ice
trembles it like some just-invented musical instrument
and that shrieking obbligato to winter
sounds like the tension in a stretched worm
when the robin has it hauled halfway out of the lawn
I stand outside
between house and outhouse
feeling my body stiffen in fossilized rigor mortis
and listening
thinking
this is the reason we built on the flood plain
damn right
the seriousness of things beyond your understanding

Whatever I have not discovered and enjoyed
is still waiting for me
and there will be time
but now are these floating stars on the freezing lake
and music fills the darkness
holds me there listening
—it's a matter of separating these instants from others
that have no significance
so that they keep reflecting each other
a way to live and contain eternity
in which the moment is altered and expanded
my consciousness hung like a great silver metronome
suspended between stars
on the dark lake
and time pours itself into my cupped hands shimmering

I

We are not alone in the world
our brothers the animals
               our sisters the birds
–at the making day they were late
and the creatures of sea and marsh
remained when We crawled away

With the host on the salt plain's edge
at the giving out of hands
they were chasing each other's tails
or sniffing each other's ass
–when the maker of land and sea
questioned about their souls
there was howling among the trees

When they handed out the blessings
and looked deep in their creatures' eyes
they responded with great unease
and could not meet that gaze

At the naming of things We know
they chirped and hissed and growled
and went with the winds of the world
–when they died their scattered bones
were forbidden the Holy Ground

Ignorant of what they are not
unaware of things that they are
their memory is lost as Eden
their anger the same as fear

To follow a trail through the forest
and not think
                    "Have I been here before?"
or remember an odd-shaped stone
that hitch-hiked to now with a glacier
from the last Ice Age
a stone reminding them of something else
and triggered a whole series of rememberings
or notice a daisy like the day's eye
déjà vu in the etymological dark
—but how do we *know* that?
Perhaps the caribou with antler antennae
in their hundreds of thousands
have stood on some primordial beach
near Great Bear Lake listening
to music from the Crab Nebula
the debris of a supernova
in a caribou fantasy
—or the arctic wolf searching
his genes all the way back to Genesis
for the Godwolf's terrible face
—at least the deer's soft helpless look
facing death wraps up that moment
for the time when we die ourselves
and the far distant eye from nowhere
peers with instinctive distaste
into our own brief lives

It was after our fathers had been listening
a long time to the rain
to birds chirping and the silence between
and they listened to the wolves
crying at night to the wolf-mother
and the glacier-spirit whispered to them
and our fathers made words
Then we looked at each other
and knew from the sounds
that came from our mouths
how the beasts were made nervous
with ears lower than their tails
when we approached them
we knew we were men

A long time after
one among us was called Lok
—when Lok fell from a tree
many sleeps ago he landed
near a bear and ran for his life
we pointed at him after that
we pointed and said Lok
When the bear returned again
we scrambled up a tree
and all of us said "Lok-Lok-Lok"
The bear was angry
and tried to climb after us
his mouth frothed foam
his claws wounded the tree
then we pointed at the bear
and the sound came again
we jumped up and down in the tree
we were very happy

For a long time after
we pointed at each other often
we said "Lok-Lok-Lok"
—and the sound changed in our heads
we could not plead with it to stay
we could not command it to go
it belonged to itself
but sometimes when things are most serious
most solemn and most important
the sound returns among us
and will not be silent
Lok himself said nothing
his face became haunted
from the sound that was his name
and was not his name any longer
he went away into the forest
and did not return
until his memory grew faint among us

For a long time after
we wondered about it
this gift that was given us
but denied the beasts
we wondered what it might mean:
—and the gods speak within us
when we least expect their voices
when we know there is no other help
Listen Listen Listen
under the moon we say his name
solemnly seriously we say his name
the man who left us and never came back
"Lok-Lok-Lok"
and the gods are listening
until the name returns from the mountains
and lives again among us

I don't know what to think about April
—sometimes a wet bitch
walking the country roads
without an umbrella
—sometimes glorious
Let's just play it by ear:
she is the drip-drip-drip
of an all-day rain
sloshing the soul
she is also the
condition of being
young we remember best
after it's over
in a life that seems
to have little meaning
except in small details
except in you and I
—a summer that began badly
springs fading in memory
full of loss
aching with loss
of something valuable
you can't remember anyway
from another existence and
"What am I doing here?"
the child wondered
—but here's April
and it's glorious

ON THE DEATH OF F.R. SCOTT
(Jan. 31, '85)

The new year continues without him
the Ides of March will pass him by
(no Caesar here important enough for murder)
Easter and its calendar Christ
crucified again on the living-room wall
and all the long hot dog-days
of summer with screaming small boys
tormenting thrilled small girls
pretending boredom
            —he will be absent then

(Now
I hear the customary eulogies
"Invaluable man"—"outstanding accomplishments"
"citizen of the mind's republic"
—but I invented that last one
and feel impatient with myself
because I'm changing from a Scott tribute
the way it started out
and become
another way of saying to myself
"I miss that man")

But the country goes on
content with incompetent leaders
the bland sleepwalkers
            and glib sellouts of Ottawa
—a man of warm feeling and nobility dies
no flags half-mast on public buildings
citizens remain calm in non-emergencies
for we exist in a special geography
            of isolation from each other
                  and fear of emotion

prefer to keep a reasonable distance
from one of our number
betraying any signs of intelligence
–but it will not be forgiven us
if a man like this is entirely wasted
another leaf fallen in a maple forest
become humus on the forest floor
and something may grow there

All obsequies are really personal
good taste precludes sackcloth and ashes
but elevators skip the 13th floor
therefore understate the power and glory
delete the Roncarelli case
omit the CCF Manifesto and the like
remember Scott at midnight in North Hatley
when I needed him and his rare
common gift of simple kindness
yes

It will be obvious of course that
I waver between eulogy and the personal
and cannot escape either
and think of Peter Dale Scott
who cannot escape either either
(the father like a hanging judge
the father like a child's idol
                –and such bitterness for both)

At least a dozen Scotts exist
–each a prosecuting attorney somewhere
fighting intolerance anti-Semitism such
blood sports of racists
by which we mark ourselves
as inescapably human
–each a defence witness as well:
include mention of that mysterious

phrase "What's right"
all ambiguous crap removed
what's fair and equitable for everyone
What's right?
Frank Scott knew

LADY

The old and much-used words
I use
when thinking of you
("luminous" is one of them)
become linked and hyphenated
their meanings multiple
they glow like seed pearls
around your throat
—words that mean flesh
change and become spirit
are so enthralled
they take on meanings
from all the other languages
English can never say
—but the metaphors fade
sound's mute servants
names of birds without the bird

—she stands before me
out of my own imagination
a phantom lady
and multiplies as flowers do
—and herself
knowing those other selves exist
may ask of their behaviour

When things get miserable for me
and I'm moaning about old age
I think of John Clare escaping
from his madhouse in Epping Forest
tramping home to Northborough
90 miles on the Great North Road
one shoe sole flapping underfoot
gravel inside the other
sleeping anywhere for three nights
no money no food and eating grass
dreaming of his old girlfriend
dead Mary Joyce he didn't know was dead
sick with sunstroke sick with hunger
sick with his own madness
Meeting his wife Patty on the road
she throwing her arms around him
and he pushing her off
not knowing it was Patty of the Vale
believing her a madwoman
—and when I think of all this
I'm a bit ashamed of myself
remembering a rural poet in 1841
John Clare
and his "Meet me in the green glen—"
trudging toward the light

When arthritis is killing me
or a bad hangover
after youth ended with a whimper
I think of D.H. Lawrence
irritated at just about everyone
his reach greater than his grasp
(an 8-inch reach with 6-inch equipment)
escaping from country to country
free from everyone except himself

in search of the sun
spitting a few drops of tubercular
blood in seaports and railway stations
DHL
in a big hurry to know the names of things
in order that his mind might touch
the things themselves
his friends the birds beasts and flowers
—and they have not forgotten him
DHL
turning to look backward
stumbling toward the light

When I'm feeling sorry for myself
(nobody loves me—boo-hoo)
I think of Vincent Van Gogh
searching the faces of the twenty-two
self-portraits he painted in Paris
to discover why all the women
he loved fled in opposite directions
Vincent
searching for the light in Arles
deep in the madness that was his sanity
hauling the moon down with a paintbrush
returning it to the sky transfigured
exploding the stars at St. Rémy
Vincent
with his mutilated ear
hobbling toward the light

I grumble peevishly
(being none of those three)
in the hangover after youth
irritated that I cannot escape myself
irritated in turn at the several
gods and devils with residence inside myself
clamouring for attention
thinking of Clare DHL and Vincent
limping toward the light.

What shall we say to Death
you and I
when time is short and breath
scant for you and I?

How can I answer Yes or No
my dear my dear
when we're far away from the cold
but near to each other here?

But what shall we say to Death
when it comes night comes
and there is no cheating it unless
we're blind and deaf and dumb?

What shall we say to Death
with Yes defeated by No
and only the winter of loving left
only the snow?

I have no answer to give you
my dear my dear
only that I *was* always with you
and I am still here

                    —to change the contour
                              of earth itself
bend a small arc of the horizon
to include this unnatural irregularity
a kind of bump
perhaps displeasing to the cultivated eye
I mean build a house
abstract a portion of the sky
place personal boundaries
on nothingness
                    —on nothingness?
—the brain reels and retracts antennae
it's like contemplating eternity or infinity
the mind can't cope
(and no buck-toothed intellectual caveman
in the pause after inventing a skin tent
would tolerate such semantic bullshit either
even before his brain-pan started to fossilize)

                    Just the same
when my wife and I built this A-frame
with a pile of second-hand lumber
and used concrete blocks from Belleville
and barn-boards from the country north of—
that's what we did
                    fenced-in the sky
I mean: the sheer grandeur of it!
(it was me what did it God)
a peg on which to hang the ego
while birds and small local animals
apply for new road maps

Occasionally
wandering my rural domain

I notice a hole in the earth
a kind of bump under the horizon
an old house foundation with maybe
rotting timbers old bricks rusty tin cans
and think
            that's what awaits us
it happens to pyramids and mud shanties
and all I can do about it
my small passion for permanence
is to stand outside at night
(conceding probability to the "Big Bang")
in the full rush and flow of worlds
dancing the firefly dance of the universe
stand on my local planet and
neighbourhood galaxy
beside my crumbling little house
inside my treacherous disappearing body
while the dear world vanishes
and say weakly
            I don't like it
            I don't like it

            —to no one who could possibly be listening

MAYBE FISH

Never to touch
the beloved
in any sense whatever:
merely hover
like green-gold
watering cans
and squirt milt
down a hole
scraped in the gravel
Divided always
by thick transparent
glass while looking
at each other
often sort of
goggling
thru dim green windows
of a weed-grown victorian mansion
where someone
someone from another era
has just softly closed the door
of the master bedroom
And the deer in the wall
tapestry yearn for each other
for century after century
divided by centimetres
of ancient cloth
—and there is something decidedly
comic about it
especially
if you're not a deer

But oh my dear
never to touch
the beloved

   never

     never

We argued about things
whether you should seek experience
or just let it happen to you
(me the former and she the latter)
and the merits of St. Paul
as against his attitude to women
(she admired him despite chauvinism)
But what pitifully few things
we remember about another person:
me sitting at her typewriter
at Elm Cottage in England
and translating her short story
"A Bird in the House" into a radio play
directly from the book manuscript
in just two or three days
(produced by J. Frank Willis
on CBC his last production)
and being so proud of my expertise
Then going away to hunt books
while my wife recuperated
from an operation
Returning to find the play finished
Margaret had taken about three hours
to turn my rough draft
into a playable acting version
fingers like fireflies on the typewriter
and grinning at me delightedly
while my "expertise" went down the drain
And the huge cans of English ale she bought
Jocelyn called "Al-size-ale"
and the people coming over one night
to sing the songs in *The Diviners*
(for which I gave faint praise)
And the books she admired—

Joyce Cary's *The Horse's Mouth*
Alec Guinness as Gulley Jimson a Valkyrie
riding the Thames on a garbage barge
—how Graham Greene knew so much
that she both loved and cussed him
for anticipating her before she got there
and marked up my copy of his essays
These are the lost minutiae
of a person's life
things real enough to be trivia
and trivial enough to have some permanence
because they recur and recur—with small
differences of course—in all our lives
and the poignance finally strikes home
that poignance is ordinary
Anyway how strange to be writing about her
as if she were not here
but somewhere else on earth
—or not on earth
given her religious convictions
Just in case it does happen
I'd like to be there when she meets St. Paul
and watch his expression change
from smugness to slight apprehension
while she considers him as a minor character
in a future celestial non-fiction novel
And this silly irrelevance of mine
is a refusal to think of her dead
(only parenthetically DEAD)
remembering how alive
she lit up the rooms she occupied
like flowers do sometimes and the sun always
in a way visible only to friends
and she had nothing else

On my workroom wall an original letter
from DHL that reads
                    "Dear M,
                              I send you
by this post, registered M.S.,
an article I did on the Indians
and the Bursum Bill" et cetera
I think he used a steel nib pen
and dipped it in ink when dry
and you can see where the nib ran
short of ink and faded the words
in his letter like *"and the"* above
Reading DHL's handwriting hypnotizes
me as Mabel Sterne and Walter Lippman
and Scofield Thayer flit past and are dead
and the New York *World* of the letter
died long ago of financial malnutrition
I read the letter and my hand reaches
for ghost ink that isn't there
just the way he did
and stop to think about this poem
I'm writing (trivial): and from
the other side of the letter
I can see its continuation there
visible thru the Taos N.M. notepaper:
"from the other side" I say
And this is what obsession does
you read meanings into nothingness
or perhaps into very little
And remember a remark by Margaret Laurence
"I expect to grow old raising
cats and roses–" (but she didn't)
When you dismiss the groping metaphysics

what all this means is a patented
method of jumping from Lawrence
to Laurence and I mourn both
from steel nib pen & ink to cats & roses
Goodbye–

FLYING OVER VANCOUVER ISLAND
(from Port Renfrew to Tofino)

turquoise–turquoise–turquoise
              in green-blue lakes below
a necklace strung together
each feeding a sister lake
farther down among the mountains
where snow melts in late spring
Incongruously
I think of an auto wrecker's yard
in my hometown of Trenton
with a necklace of Ford-Chev-Plymouth parts
jumbled and compressed together
into a nameless bundle by machines
waiting to leap violently outward
and produce a Frankenstein auto
–then snow & turquoise lakes & Cessna aircraft
and myself are all jumbled together
in my limited little mind
where space is at a premium
–joined later by a wrecked freighter
breaking apart slowly on coastal rocks
once loaded with Dodge Colts from Japan
(the pilot tells me)
which disappeared right after the wreck
winched off by local gremlins

We land at Tofino in water
and for a few minutes after
the town is invisible to me
my mind having zigzagged from Ameliasburg
and Trenton and Toronto to Vancouver
to here from sixty years ago
and a great blinding sheet of–
and ultraviolet X-rays irradiate with–

and I am suffering from self-inflicted wounds
and turquoise Turquoise TURQUOISE
sing in my brain like the variable
components of love Love LOVE

–in a Frankenstein poem

80 years old is young for a writer,
especially here in Canada;
and you, having visited the City of Light,
revisit your own youth again and again.

Meeting you once in Toronto
for lunch with Bob Weaver, the day after
a young burglar had come and gone
from your house: thinking of laughter

at the Four Seasons hearing the story
about you and that burglar reeling
around the living room, and your
fighting him off: the tremendous glee
in your face at him running away–

I grew up with MacLennan and Callaghan,
and meeting you was meeting an icon;
but at the Four Seasons no brass band,
only Elwood Glover and his microphone.

I wanted to say that I understand
your feelings about Hemingway in Paris,
about Fitzgerald and McAlmon,
the enthusiasm of it, the caring

for something outside you: the knowledge
that writers are all closely related,
but some more than others, an allegiance
exceeding mere words on the page.

I wanted to say I was a hero worshipper
as well, in Montreal, in '57,

when I slept on Irving Layton's floor,
he was an iconoclast too, he was Hem.

At least for me. And Dudek was McAlmon,
the encourager of other men's words;
and Frank Scott, lean and magisterial,
he was fat Ford Madox Ford.

Faces and figures of course are different,
but they were archetypes and absolutes,
and I felt for them the same affection:
altho Montreal wasn't quite so beautiful

as Paris, yet it had the same ferment
of writers and their marvellous egos.
My Place du Dôme was smoked meat at Ben's.
Your Paris eventually became Toronto.

Well, our sojourn in these "lighted places"
ends: the heroes resemble Odysseus,
who got lost on his way home. Lights fade,
crescendos tail off to a minor key–

You were never lost, kept finding yourself,
and being found by people like Wilson,
Bob Weaver and others, kept ringing the bell
for round two with burglars next season.

But remember our mutual pantheon
–and what we felt quite unashamedly
for them was love, for brothers, for friends,
Layton-Hemingway, Dudek-McAlmon.

And Montreal as the City of Light?
It isn't even incongruous for me.
I hope it isn't for you–the bright
memory that replaces all things eventually...

All except such things as words,
perishable words, scribbled on paper.
And Morley, my best wishes for this anniversary:
live long, live well, remember the future,
your friends tomorrow, your friends today.

In the judgement of aficionados
the home run or strikeout
leaping catch at the fence
these are the adrenaline criteria
of what it's all about

But the game is puzzling
this year's pennant winners last next year
great players gone mediocre
—yes I know
nothing in life is certain

But there are moments of such stillness
in the game
                silence much less than silence
(like at a lynching when a black guy
stares long at a white or when
power fails during an electrocution)
and in the silence:
a hundred years have gone by
and everyone here is long dead
Reagan is dead Mulroney is dead
everyone now alive has forgotten them
until a banjo .120 hitter smacks a homer
then a great sigh from the stands
and wind roars between planets

If there really is a heaven baseball
certainly must be played there
and if there's a hell there too
and they play a universal World Series
every aeon or millenium or so
when Babe Ruth gets sick again on hot dogs
and Dizzy Dean drunk on celestial beer

Ted Williams pops up and tips his hat (sometimes)
where everything that happened keeps happening
and all that we dreamed we love
is still true when we wake up
Well—if it ain't that way it oughta be
and either way there was always You
sitting next to me or in bed or somewhere
nearby while the Game goes on and on—

1

A commonplace of the season
these sky hieroglyphs
cobwebs in the clouds
during October
when they change from nouns to verbs
homebodies to wanderers
and excitedly in the sky
call out directions
then head for somewhere
they've never been before
no place prepared for them
at the ends of the earth

2

What shall we leave behind
that means anything?
—some feathers
our children
a great many of them perhaps
but they have no memory of us
not for very long
—in any event
the memory of yourself in others
is not a reward for dying
nor the long sleep
in which we become
everything we could imagine

A music no Heifetz or Paganini knew
it never occurred to them there could be
—at night when man-sounds fade
and shadows pretend to be shadows
the lake is trying to decide about itself
whether it is better to be ice or water
and can't make up its mind
it yearns toward both of them
And little two-inch tubular crystals form
phantoms in the water
—when the merest hint of wind comes
they *sing*
they sing like nothing here on earth
nothing here on earth resembles this
this inhuman yearning for something other
sighing between the planets

On earth
I have manoeuvred myself near them
my face close to the crystal hexagons
kneeling uncomfortably
on this rocky shoreline near Ameliasburg
temperature 32 degrees Fahrenheit
shining my flashlight on them
trying to observe the exact instant
water stops being water
becomes uncertain about what it is
trembling
it shivers and questions itself until
until the ice-amoeba in the world's veins
sings in midnight silence

I can't stand the cold
run back into the house to escape it

you watching at the window
questioning me:
"What happened out there?"
−kneeling on the rocky headland
remembering something left behind
shivering a little in the bedroom
my cold hexagons and your warm flesh
refusing to come together
and the cry of one lost animal
wandering the frozen shoreline
wanting to be everything
and silence
and sleep

SPRINGTIME
(after Housman)

All the springs unite with this one
both the first one and the last
when the birds are winged flowers
and the flowers are singing birds

Every sunup's like a birthday
every sundown promised more
there are candles lit for noonday
and the darkness shines with stars

As for dying—when it's over
there'll be time to make a fuss
—but for now there's love and laughter
and the springtime is for us

GRADATIONS

In the measurements of my life
I take pleasure in their decline
observing inevitable changes
counting the moments left

And this is not gallows humour
an exercise in morbidity
it's using what's left the best way
in order that crumbs will taste like cake

—an exploration of limited time
a wary circling of infirmities
so much like dangerous beasts
to make them at least partly useful
as they are to me in this poem

—all joyful things in their departure
must be replaced with something different
in their quietness an implicit shout
all the strangenesses be made familiar
and pain become a silent banner

I have reached this place alone
and remain alone with no one watching
boredom finally ended
tyrannies of the flesh still bearable
and expecting something marvellous

IN THE DESERT
–for Milton Acorn

My friends die off one by one:
and far away in the desert
caravans are plodding thru the sand
I can see them at the horizon's edge
the young on their many roads to Mecca
but I have been there often
and returned again

My friends die off:
far distant in waste places
the living move in many directions
I could run after them shouting
across the desert "Wait for me–"
And sometimes I have done that
but things went badly for me
and rushing to meet those people
excited and panting
their faces change into someone else
their faces change...

This morning
wandering the grey desert
looking for a cactus flower
with caravans moving in the distance
sinking under grey horizons
I noticed someone moving in the shadows
coming toward me at a great pace
and they cried out as I had done
"Wait for me–"

A single figure
but impossible to say
whether it was male or female
crossing the sand dunes shouting

arriving where I stand waiting
in a great flurry of dust and sand:
it was someone I did not know
and very young
I was about to say in a neutral voice
"You had better go back–"

But looking into that eager face
and hopeful eyes–: I glimpsed the flux
of what exists and does not yet exist
a wavering between disappointment and joy
and knew there was only a moment left
before the little gap in time healed itself
I said welcome
and knew this messenger from the desert
was someone I had been waiting for
and clasped them in my arms
the stranger

Tasting with both your eyes
hearing with all your blood
as if you'd been listening
a very long time in fact
for some hundred million years
when flowers first arrived
in the waste places of earth
the bright trumpets of April
announcing themselves to God

In some misty Cretaceous valley
dinosaurs glopped around
suddenly caught the scent
snuffling stupid not knowing
they had only thirty-five
million more years to live
Mammals chattered excitedly
forgetting opal and vair
of the sun's heraldic birth
then rushed to tell their wives
how intelligent they were
And everyone who was still
undecided about being born
changed their minds fast
and materialized from nothing
as all miracles do

In a cold Cretaceous valley
all that long ago winter
the little hairy mammals
huddled together for warmth
waiting to become human
stared hopelessly at each other

while earth prepared that summer
for an additional miracle
this time a coloured one
as if a child had clapped his hands
for yellow yellow yellow

Each generation keeps trying
to explain to the next generation
how terrified we all are
of something that can't be explained
and keep talking and talking around–
as if talking will delay indefinitely
whatever it is we are afraid of

The closest you can get
is that the explanation involves being human
which of itself cannot be adequately explained
except to say that as human beings
having a beginning and middle and end
we are born we live and we die

In the beginning
we don't know where we came from
apart from our most recent ancestors that is
and in the end
after a million years or so of being dust
we don't know where we're going to
only in the middle
do we have some control over things

Walking a tightrope over Niagara Falls say
the beginning middle and end of the rope
are all present simultaneously
except that the middle and end are interchangeable
in that context
              and looking down
instead of my drowned and crushed body
I see a fine mist floating upward
holding in its greyness a faint rainbow
rising from the gorge to meet my ancient dust

In the middle of things my future dust
hears itself make a small cry
and after a million years or so
when your own dust may be listening
the ghost decibels sound their chimes
and a planet of inconceivable heaviness
moves fractionally to make this possible
and a small rain like tears
that can only be imagined by lovers
who do not yet exist
is falling somewhere

II

On Sunday the Christian holiday
Buddhists come to the park
and I walk there too
neither Buddhist nor Christian
The little boy dolls in uniform
troop solemnly to the cenotaph
the little girl dolls are solemn too
standing at Sadako's statue
& mama san & papa san & all the kids
& dozens of grandparents
come here laughing to have a picnic
all enjoying themselves as
hard as they can
for it's 1971 and won't be long
everything merry as a marriage bell
that rings between birth and death
the only one you can hear at all well
Now a geisha
or what I take to be one
goes by as beautiful as spring rain
wearing a silk kimono sighing
and I think of following her
but hell I don't really care
Ceremonies continue all over the place
in the midst of which a ten-
year-old girl comes up
to me and says "Please what's the time?"
I tell her and she holds out
her hand for me to shake politely
and I shake it and
the Yomiuri Giants are playing the
Chunichi Dragons at the ball park today
The Bomb was twenty-six years ago
and thinking

about the contrast between old and new
only on television do
magicians and samurai survive
stride thru tall bamboo forests
ineradicable as termites
—magicians play the county fairs
making strange ur-r-r sounds
in their throats they leap fifty
feet straight up in the air not
Superman men but talented
and hypnotize damn near everybody
—samurai search for their lost leader
whom they never knew at all well
unemployed fighting men
so brave they scare themselves
and shave without looking at the mirror
Well the point of all this eludes me
but if there is a point to something
I prefer that little girl
asking the time and offering her hand
to shake like a 16th century lady
at a court ceremony honouring the Korean ambassador
whom I have not met and may never
me the large awkward fifty-year-old barbarian
with unsung children and tone-deaf wife
from the land beyond the west wind
I bend over that small hand
making a strange er-r-r sound in my throat
like when I was a shy stuttering child
afraid of dark blue policemen
and when I grow up I shall marry her

Hiroshima

SCOTT HUTCHESON'S BOAT
–for Angus Mowat

"A fishing boat" Angus says
"should not be too soft on the bilge
have too much sheer or too
much speed for the job–"
"Angus" I say "we should all have too
much of whatever it is we ain't–"

One grey Sunday Angus
found the skeleton
on a sand beach of Scott
Hutcheson's boat built in 1910
the same he saw being born
when he was a very young man
Angus mentions beauty
the line and sweep of a boat
that sailed 58 years
with three different skippers
and stopped working to die
Then Angus found it again
derelict in 1968
and tore it apart lovingly
piece by piece tenderly
a romance of wood and flesh
he measured every nuance
of the way it met the waves
and for five years of building
the boat danced in his brain
–he "copied" another man's thoughts
probed in a dead man's mind
"But it's only a copy" Angus says
that stands in his boat shed now
in 1973
Angus for god's sake man
get off this beauty crap

Hutcheson is a thought of a thought
his hewing axe quaint in your mind
his adze rusted and gone
remembered slightly by you
Of course he built the best he could
and you did too
with "not too much speed for the job"
everything heart-rendingly the same
(except it isn't 1910 any longer
and it isn't now either because you couldn't stay
but nobody can because of the darkening weather)
a boat worn useful as a road or an old habit
parts replaceable but damn near eternal
wood paint nails canvas all things you can touch
plus something you only know is there
because you can touch nothing only feel it
as others have in their random lives
and reached for whatever they thought was nearest
but the thing danced off and they looked away
at paint and nails and wood and canvas
                    −how the outline blurs
from hollow log to Egyptian raft
galleys and guffas and crude pirogues
till the triremes come with great bronze rams
to beat the seas into foaming red
while oarsmen strain at the roots of time
and the quick are dead and the dead grow hands
At which point maybe I'm lost myself
having skippered your ark over mountaintops
taken the idea you think is Scott
Hutcheson's boat
                    but it ain't
−the thing is boat & Hutcheson & Angus
and a fourth is me hanging around
for something to write about
and maybe some other ghosts
We're haunted by more than our deaths
we're plagued with those other lives

and our lives are copied from life
–how the Mediterranean coast
looms near in the cold grey fog
the goat skins brim with wine
and high wind sings in the sails–
Well Angus what the hell
I think you contain them all
(it wasn't this other guy only)
Hutcheson his boat yourself
and myself in the same net
the long human sweep of things
call it continuity I guess
for lack of another word
where we have been
where we are going
and you can get your ticket here
in sun and water and words
disappearing like foam
–but knowing what we do
and leaving ourselves behind
skeletons on the beach
dead but pre-knowing we're there
till someone like Angus or me
copies Scott Hutcheson's boat
far from this Quinte shoreline
and the blueprints read like this
and it damn well better be right

Enough cracked ice for a billion cocktails
sled dogs running along the beach
like golfers searching for a lost ball
Leah and Regally waving goodbye
as the motor stutters into blue water
on the road of the killer whales
with mile-long icebergs drifting south
and behind us the lost island
Jonahsie wears a terylene shirt
           grins at me
where I shiver inside a parka
And I think about our relationship
of mutual curiosity for two weeks
Jonahsie the basic and primary hunter
with other attributes secondary
he must be hunter to become husband and father
and human to be either
crouched over pretending to be a caribou
           rifle ready on the tundra
or crawling behind cloth camouflage to shoot seal
growing old in the white land
           as we all grow older
I am seized with dramatic melancholy
for the young man in his early twenties
soon to be middle-aged as myself
But I can't be sad long in this sunlight
like cold yellow beer
           and the bow wave
spattering blue ocean in my face
           I think of the old ones
Dorsets who lived here when Christ was crucified
and Thule people gone three hundred years
whalers   traders   explorers
           I feel like a procession

But here is my turning point
these familiar islands once so strange
"Foxe his farthest" and Purdy his most
but the planets are receding
the arrow with its delicate balance
has thumped against the horizon

At Pang I pay Jonahsie by pre-arrangement
the money embarrassing both of us
and we shake hands
                              his brown face already strange
I stand in the mud with my baggage
thinking of that island among the ice
in the deep blue of Cumberland Sound
with its white whales and ring seals
                              –feeling like Alexander Selkirk
                              who left his island
but Crusoe stayed there
among the goats and sled dogs
and will never come back

Kikastan Islands and Pangnirtung, Baffin

Riding the back of a bucking jeep
thru the Sierra Maestra Mountains
holding onto the canvas hoping
we don't leave the earth altogether
and red dust of Cuba
seeps into clothes and hands and faces
—like riding thru an earth sunset
and lights in the dust are people's eyes
Pigs asleep on the road run squealing
chameleon lizards by the roadside
palm-thatched huts in heat haze
and the sea a thin line of blue lace
white-edged perhaps 25 miles away
The jeep driver must be a madman
we just miss a team of oxen
once we nearly hit a truck
our small red cloud and its big sunset
join like dusty diarrhoea
with scarlet Spanish curses
and the jeep blushes

Pilon on the sea coast
dusty small town like a movie set where
man and boy clop past on a Hollywood nag
and hitchposts all over the place
We stand in dust and wait for Gary Cooper
who turns out to be the sugar mill manager
and shows us the damaged buildings
where a sea raider opened up two days
back with shellfire wounding a pig and
hitting a woman in the buttocks with splinters
destroying the sugar warehouse
making a million dollar bonfire
of mountainous slag sugar

Now a tall gold-
toothed Negro with a longshoreman's
hook climbs over the slag heaps grinning
and the sun breaks his face into pieces
of light

The road back:
rain falling in the mountains
a hot rain making pockmarks in mooncountry
or it would be except for soaring royal palms
the live smell of red earth rising
to your nostrils like animal urine
decayed flowers and tidal marshes
the not unpleasant smell of Cuba
so rank and fertile you think the jeep
might sprout roots if you ever stopped
if you ever stopped
and your arms are tired rubbery tentacles
holding onto the reeling bucking planet
as the insomniac jeep
plunging thru wheel ruts
takes you back where you came from

Pilon, Cuba

Between the Street of the Barbers and
the Street of the Tinsmiths in
Mexico City lived a girl who wished
            who wished
                        to be beautiful—
Consuelo
with the coppery blood of the Aztecs
and a raping Spanish foot soldier
disabled at Otumba and left behind by
Cortez to father bastards and produce
after 500 years
                  plain Consuelo—

Her mirror is the rain barrel
outside the *vecindad*
in which she looks every morning
                  without much hope
and the dark place on her throat
that the sun touches is not gold
or costume jewellery of any value
to collectors of rare and beautiful things—

Consuelo of the Aztecs with
also
thin Spanish blood as indirect result
of marked courtesy of an Amer—
            uh Spanish
            foot soldier—
She has nothing to leave behind
            when she dies
but things in the rain barrel
which have little value to anyone
no goldbrooch   manscalps   minkfur   glassjewels

Look down
in the mirror
that wavers and changes
from water to sky and back to water again
the heart of the water is unbroken
for 500 years–
Now her sisters come
in the morning
yawning and scratching a little
with red flowers in their hair
to look at themselves
look past themselves in the water
deep
in the velvet centre
where the silence is unbroken
and think of Consuelo who was not beautiful–

I am getting water for my wife's tea
& passing by in the corridor
notice this boy sitting on a bed
around 7:30 in the morning
and pause for some reason
at the steam-bath day's beginning
I glance in the half-open door
the boy is absolutely lost and dreaming
his family swirling around him
getting ready to leave
Coming back I pass the same door
again with a full water jug
the boy is still nowhere
a place I've visited
myself back or ahead in time
now being only a filter
as it seems to be for him
I'm tempted to say "Hello" or "Goodbye"
but the boy is eloquently silent
so positively negatively absent
his coloured shape
is all he's left behind
But I can't stop anyway
my wife wants her tea-water
and I can't speak Spanish either
so what the hell
But I think what I think
he's thinking sending himself
out to make a coloured chart
of what the world is
deciding whether it's interesting
sending his absent self back
into the 18th century
Spanish fort across the harbour

mouth his bright Toledo sword
lopping a pirate's ear off in 1723
Or maybe in 1990 or so
muy caballero in a boudoir
or government office finding
jobs and social assistance
for starving Indians maybe
The boy's random self
can do anything in fact
everything is a story
he can join at any point
nothing began and nothing ends
(Cortez tramps the mountain plain
still searching for Montezuma
Aztecs stare at the sun's white blood
and stars drown in sewers
white men drink their dollar death
in city jungles dead on the cross
God might happen to anyone
where the moon inflates with a bicycle pump
the U.S. space age grinds to a halt)
But I can't speak to the boy
over the edge of time was
he has passed my death
and not reached his own
around 2030 A.D. maybe
the language has changed too
I can't say good morning
to him in his language
but at least now I know
the reason for this uncanny feeling
if we had glanced at each other
I would have seen his
small face with an expression
I once had coming back slowly
from where we've never been
to places we can't return to
And I pick my thoughts up

one by one and take them
where paper is and write
while my wife makes tea
After which we get into the car
and drive north
over the dry and hungry land
of desert and mountains

Mexico

No way of knowing where we went
on those long journeys
Sometimes there was a whiteness
as of snow that obscured everything
but it wasn't snow
Sometimes it seemed we left a campfire
and looking for it again
couldn't even find the burned place
blundering into the trees and buildings
but then nothing
has ever confused me as much as light
Sometimes we arrived back separately
but still seemed inside the borders
we crossed by accident
and want to be there if we think it real
but we do not think it real
There is one memory
of you smiling in the darkness
and the smile has shaped the air
                    around your face
someone you met in dream
has dreamed you waking

Drinking beer with three men
I haven't seen since school days
They ask me about myself
I mention going to Cuba last year
along with ten other Canadians
riding a jeep thru the Sierra Maestras
to a coast town where sea raiders
opened up with shellfire on a sugar mill
in Camaguay Province two days before
A tall negro with a longshoreman's hook
climbing the burned black slag heaps grinning
the sun breaking his face into pieces of light
On the way home
stranded in Mexico City four days
My old schoolmates don't believe me
(Okay I got a little carried away
but I didn't even tellem about that gal
half a block from the hotel in Havana
I'm on my way to get cigarettes
she just looks at me with yellow eyes
and I can't put my foot down for 3½ seconds
I knew how long from the skipped heartbeats
when she released me I was middle-aged
and found wanting)
One guy talks about the Mackenzie River
where he says he worked one summer
and they don't believe him either
and damned if I know for sure
whether he did work on the Mackenzie River
Another tells of going thru
the Connaught Tunnel in a boxcar
during the Depression
and mountains like silver spoons in blue sky
Of course they don't believe him either

his eyes fixed 20 years back in yellow beer
and it might be true
But the amazing thing is here we are
sitting together and drinking beer
and thinking the others terrible liars
which is unbelieveable to me in itself
And from the way these guys talk I know
this sort of thing happens
every time they get together
it's ordinary and commonplace
that we're all liars
(I love you I love you—let's fuck!)
and I'm scared I'm scared
For some reason tears come
into my eyes
perhaps thinking of them next day
when dawn comes
                    their wives
their jobs and failures
themselves brooding among beer bottles
if one lie fails they invent another
to support the first and reality
is a grey place in the jigsaw
map of the world
they haven't thought of yet
and I'm scared I'm scared
as the world a better liar invented
fades at my elbow

I get up to leave and lie and say
          "Good seeing you again"
And they believe me they believe me
I wonder what I've missed seeing
near closing time at this hotel
in a sad small town

Trenton

BEER POEM

Think of beer as liquid gold
think of it as curse or blessing?
Years ago I thought of it as
Damocles' sword hung over my kidneys
when myself and two friends
(since deceased) had 15 gallons
working in an oak whisky barrel
another 15 gallons maturing in bottles
plus 15 gallons all ready to drink
It required deep thought
not to mention lightning decisions
neither of which am I capable of:
15 gallons ready every five days
and we had to drink it all every five days
on accounta we didn't have enough bottles
to stem the onrushing tide of beer
(the mathematics are complicated)
It was then I decided Greek tragedy
most resembles Canadian comedy
in a way no Greek ever anticipated
to drink or not was never the question
to drink sufficiently the definite answer
which has always eluded my capacity
if not my understanding
The 90-degree turn or parabola
reversing the mediocre field
I grew in was always my sole intention
to live in such a way madmen
shake their heads at my psychosis
my grace my chutzpah whatchamacallit
my epitaph a movement melting into morning
and morning into evening moving
in such a way to become what someone
inside myself says I cannot thus

to arrive and depart in a great circle
—which is to say
when I am one with the ancient Egyptians
who stored beer in their pyramids
for edification and consumption of the dead
when I am one with the waving fields
sharing ritual death and rebirth of barley
and the mould and amino acids and one
with the building blocks of earth
but sharing a last drink with friends
long after closing time . . .

Do not die
for if you do
then I shall have no use for women
but that's a lie
they're in my blood and you are too
you most of all of them
and a hunger to say the unsayable
a dream a drink a choice of something
beyond the eyes' closed circuit here
a chance only
a small one
And I repeat the previous instructions
that is–in the positive sense–survive
nor ever rejoice in the idea of death
as escape from anything
there is no escape from anything
not a single damn thing
Blood deals in blood
and love is never less than blood
it deals in truth & treachery & lies
it deals in life & death
but all those big words need transfusions
without blood to colour them red
So I don't understand Tristan and Isolde very well
I don't know much about those others
whoever it was swam the Hellespont
or that lost monk and nun chastely
marooned in the Middle Ages
far from the needle point of Belleville, Ont.
I don't in fact understand myself sometimes
and the schoolmaster in my dreams dreams
of life and death as a choice of things
I wake up cold and sweating
There is no choice except the grave

but a little prior to that
shortly before what happens happens
a prelude so to speak
of something drumming in the blood
of something roaring in the silence
so much like triumph
it sounds like an overture